AF244015

path

Cutting a new way or
following a well-worn
track, when either
choice is a good idea.
Looking out for signs
that might indicate
food, shelter, safety,
companionship.
Or just an
adventure...
Trying to insist on
originality, or satisfy
ambition, by going
to out of reach,
unmapped places.
Finding courage,
protective boots, the
torch of curiosity, to
go into the dark.
Lacking a sense of
direction, a timetable,
a compass.
Learning to love
dead ends.

BANG
BANG
BANG

We were out in the woods on a lovely hot day, when SUDDENLY it started HAILING! We got really cold and wet — I looked up and saw a bit of metal! So we ran and sheltered under it

Connor. Corby

Martin~
KETTERING
I really like being outdoors —
I bike to college in Kettering,
what I love best is to hear the
birds singing.

Rick, Corby

I grew up in these woods — they were my playground! A few years ago I was talking with some other people in the Boating Lake Café here — all people who cared about the woods — in the end we met regularly — and decided we'd like to clean up the woods — after setting up the "FRIENDS OF" group we got some funding to spend 10 weeks doing a DEEP CLEAN

We shifted out 27.5 TONNES of RUBBISH out of the woods! Burnt out cars and pretty much everything else you could think of.....

I dont like the woods cos they're HUGE and take a long time to walk through.
Ryan, Corby

I'm the daughter of a timber
merchant. There was always the
smell of sawdust and freshly cut wood
when I was growing up. One time
a few years ago, I was in Ghana, and
that smell!! I was in a yard where
these guys were sawing through some
tree trunks — the smell alone transported
me instantly to Gloucestershire!

Hilary

I come from Andalucia, in Spain -
we dont have so much forest there -
I love the forest here - and the
weather! I love the cold - I
like the
rain -
I just
goo
out
and get
wet!
Victor, THRAPSTON

Gaye, Weldon
Me and my twin sister were walking in the woods looking for her cocker spaniel when I felt something hit me on the shoulder. I walked a bit further and another thing hit me. I looked up and there were 2 squirrels throwing acorns right at me and Joy!

PETER, Corby

I grew up in a street backing onto the woods and all the kids in the houses more or less lived in that wood — WE WERE "THE ARROWHEAD GANG!

One day one of our number was stung by a wasp — we decided to take our revenge... We took our 'staffs', our bows and arrows and a big net — we planned to throw the net over the nest once we'd found it. Well we surrounded the nest & waited — the wasps started coming out — WE THREW THE NET OVER THEM AND STARTED ROUTING THEM — banging our feet & our staffs! Only the holes in the net were BIG — so the wasps buzzed through them and ATTACKED US! Every one of us was stung & stung — one friend — on the end of his... well... where you dont want to get stung! me & another friend saw him through his window & he was applying a raw cut onion to it — I dont think that was the right remedy!

When you look up in the woods the trees and branches make all kinds of shapes. The Shadows make shapes as well, of people and animals. I like it when the trees meet over the path and make a tunnel

Randal, Geddington–
I'm from Southern Africa – and I still
run safaris there – horse safaris.
Eight people is about the right quantity.
Do you know which other animal a
horse is scared of? – An ostrich!

One of the most enjoyable things on
these safaris is galloping with a
herd of zebras. But it's all great –
on horseback is the best way to go on
safari.

me and two of my best friends
were out walking in the woods when we saw some elves at the bottom of one of the trees. We saw them dancing a samba - they invited us to join in.
Alex. Corby

undergrowth

We are common as nettles, horrid and yet attractive, easily a mess, tangled and full of our own impenetrable secrets, secrets we hide even from ourselves. We are twisted, we trip ourselves up, yet we feed the caterpillars and host the butterflies that emerge. The animals within us conduct entire parallel lives to our own, parading as the unconscious.

We used to 'camp' in a run down cottage on Dartmoor - dropped off for weekends by my friend Penny's parents - one time we were huddled in there making toast & there was a KNOCK AT THE DOOR! It was a copper - police had the place surrounded - it was the day Mad Frankie Fraser had escaped from prison and they thought the smoke rising from the chimney might be his!
KATE, Corby

We had a naked cyclist in the woods at one point. It was Marge that reported him to the police... well you have to dont you?

"Was he wearing boots?" they asked "I wasn't looking at his feet" said Marge.

Brenda, Corby

Our second child was
actually conceived in the
woods! At 41 I was worried
that I wouldnt get pregnant
again. We were staying at my
mother in law's, and as is usual
there, we'd drunk too much. I knew
it was a fertile time in my cycle
so I grabbed my husband and
took him out to the wilds
outdoors. It was fun, though I'd
always prefer a bed! Zia, rounds

Sometimes I like
foxes and sometimes
I dont like them.
I'd be scared they might bite my bum!
Sometimes dogs bite robbers bottoms.
We have two dogs and a new puppy
called SPIDER!

Cass, fermynwoods —

It's a bit eerie in the woods at night on your own – all the sounds are magnified – even a hedgehog rustling can sound STRANGE and HUGE

Peter, Kingswood, Corby.

I was telling a friend about my job cleaning the cottages up in Fermynwoods and I was saying how I had to clean the loos — when she came up with me one day

she was surprised it was a real house as she'd imagined a tiny toilet cubicle surrounded by impenetrable brambles in the middle of the woods! Sophie Brigstock

A few years ago I caught
sight of a man camped
out here, in Kingswood. I
waited till I was out of
earshot — then rang the police.
They rang me later to thank me. He was someone they'd been
looking for for a long time. Brenda, Corby

Alison, Northampton

My parents were very strictly against me having a boyfriend - which meant we had to find secret places and ways to meet, so as a teenager I didn't go to the woods to admire the trees, but I did find out about my nature - making love in the bluebells!

We were doing a project with another arts organisation in Northumbria - all about the forest - and hanging mirrors & other reflective surfaces in the trees. We came across a boy who'd been camping here a few nights, he'd fallen out with his family & girlfriend. We got talking and did a deal. He ended up helping on the project and also let me pick him and his camping stuff up in my car and give him dinner, and take him to the Bridge - where they soon helped him find a place & get on to a training scheme.....Kate, Corby

I'd seen plenty
of adult badgers
but in the spring
every evening I'd
see this
baby
badger
just
leading
me
up the
track

a black and white
ball of fluff — Paul, FERMYN WOODS

We used to start fires in
the woods behind the supermarket
me and two older boys. Once the smoke
got so thick it covered the football pitch
next door. - Graham, Great Doddington

the only time I went into the woods
was on the way to school, I had two friends to
walk with - we'd call for each other in the morning
I wouldn't walk through the woods by myself

Debbie, Corby.

It's quite weird in the woods - so very quiet - Hannah was scared of the
ow ow
ow
Stinging nettles - so I was batting them down and pretending to be Wonder Woman
Ruth Corby

shrub layer

Middle sized trees amongst other middle sized trees growing together: gregarious,

tolerating, admiring the quirks in neighbouring shrubs of the same or different species.

thinking in the short to medium term, finding support in predictable patterns, regular doses of water and light

— finding the miraculous in the ordinary: like every day bird song, spring, the infinite variety of fellow leaves.

I like working in the woodlands
we often have a fire, sit around
the logs get the storm kettle
crackling, eat lunch, have
our tea,   PAUL

We come here every day, as therapy - since my husband's health has deteriorated we come here to keep him mobile. It gives us such a lot of ENERGY!
Myra, Thrapston

Alison WOLLASTON

I've been working with kids with learning difficulties about 15 years – my favourite thing is bringing them to the WOODS! I'm so proud of all the work they've done –

there's a transformation after they've worked hard – in the woods and in the kids themselves they come out of their shells.

I'm a bee keeper too! I just love being outside!

We were camping — three families, with 9 boys under 9 (you can imagine how relaxing that is!) WHAT I LOVED was this big old fir tree like Mother Nature, that the boys disappeared into... Laughing, climbing, playing under its leafy skirts — It really touched me and reminded me of growing up. Annabel, BRIGSTOCK

I cant go into the woods!
There's no signal!
Kitty,
BRIGSTOCK

We love playing by the stream - swinging on the rope swing throwing a ball for our dog Frankie, looking for fish
Millie
Erin
Freya
Titchmarsh

About fifteen years ago, when
I first saw this place - these
cottages were derelict, & me and
my friends peered in....
"Aah - we'd love to live here" we sighed
when I started seeing Paul we
used to talk about this place -
when it came up for rent we
just had to move here.
DREAMS REALLY CAN COME TRUE!
Claire, Fermyn Woods

A woman and her daughter
were asking where they could
buy the wood —
'Broughton House!'
I said — they
deliver!'...
'Does it spit?' asks the woman
'Listen, we cut it down — we
dont teach it manners!'
Ray

my friends sometimes ask me
when I'll move back to London
but I like running barefoot
in the woods —

Once I was running for about
two hours and I saw some blobby, shaggy
dark animals who I momentarily saw as
wolves, but they were young deer. We
ran together for about fifteen minutes!

James, Ringstead

Marian, Corby
We went out in dressing-up
gear, pretending to be Cagney
and Lacey! We played in the woods
all the time.

RRRR!
Heathcliff did try and
stick the leaves back on
the trees!
Jenny & Heathcliff, Corby

There's a twisty hazel coppice - and
they've been clearing some of it -
it's become a bit of a place for
people to build dens.

We go there on the weekends
and take bits from other kids dens
knowing ours won't last either!
The other week we saw one with
an actual PORCH!

Juliet
BRIGSTOCK

What I like working in the woods - is the teamwork
and lifting the wood - moving all the big logs!
Katherine Wellingborough

When we used to drive past these
stones, my mum would say
"I wish I had a penny for every time
I got a good hiding for tearing my
knickers on that stone!"

Ann, Brigstock

I really like coppicing - and being in the woods -
we learn how to use the saws and loppers
it makes me happy - because it's hard but I'm good at it!
Aiden, CORBY

we went up to the scout huts in
the woods with another family
and everyone got drunk — except me
because I was pregnant. So I had to
be fire marshal, while they all drank
hot chocolate with Baileys in, and scared
each other senseless over all the noises
we could hear: NIGHT IN THE FOREST

Jenny, Thrapston

My sister Sandy wasn't very well, so I invited her to come and stay - "have a rest" I said -

I took her children out to the woods and we had a lovely time splashing in puddles. When we were all tired I tried to find where I'd parked the car - but NO! We were LOST! Eventually thank goodness we made it back home.

Becky Weldon
One day recently we'd come out to set up the work party here, in the wood and we were in the landrover, & Peter said 'look at that!' It was a bush FULL OF BULLFINCHES! Hopping about, fleeting, in the spindly bush

poems

Forest of Experience

It's a flophouse for moths
they flail in beige stupor
all eyes and faintings
Victorian ladies with the vapours

I tune my ear
to their sighs
floating up in snatches
from hazy gilded blades.

Car salesman newt zips
in and out of his slovenly
basketwork: rotted black twigs
laced with bark ribbons.

A glowing toadstool
in coral polyester
sponges me
her beauty tips.

My forest of experience cracks
under the books I've read
the words I've spilt
and pictures that I've made

so badly, so laboriously.
My painting arm remembers
Prussian Blue, Chrome yellow –
squeezed from tubes

crude globs, unlike this life
where ferny fountainheads
prise lids off every shade
from eau-de-nil to sludge

and nodding fronds of fronds
swish me like a sap
into their losing green.
Nouveau pines

rise smooth as vaulting
in my restless cinema
and up in the spaghetti
canopy, sinuous capillaries

make grids for clouds
and trap me in a silence test.
Strain, for what?
Your ghost? A hare?

But only midges jitter
provincial, repetitious
have they not seen lipstick before?
Their dots itch every inch

of me, tiny tireless clubbers
mobbing the street.
Through tough foliage
glimpse bolts of deer

shaded in private fur
impervious to sting
or stinging remark –
every day there's carnage.

Bird spangled branches
trumpet fat green notes
filling all imagined spaces
in between parked stars.

A tiny dandelion bud
sucks in its yellow cheeks –
I'm the jam and you're
the butter dripping sun

it's easy to lie down
in blackthorn studded mud.

The Opposite of Sunlight

Barbed cage
of boughs
throws strobes –
spins night from
bourgeois day.

Moss radiates
holy green zeal
as it licks the floor;
and the pallid one –
lichen – pats

milky jade blobs
up the elbows of twigs
like nicotine patches
for light addicts
needing a fix.

The Remote Hut They Put Me Up In

MORNING

The walls? Magnolia. With those
PVC windows, and cheap

blinds that buckle when you tug
their plastic bobble strands.

Outside: a thousand trampolining
warblers in watercolour on the one tree.

Leaf sized birds and bird sized leaves.
Circus of flames: it is the Tree of Life.

Grey and yellow brushwork birds
swish loosely whistled songs; print

their plumped up profiles blink by blink
make every scrappy hour rococo chintz.

NOON

Cramped kitchen – slow electric rings
and humming fridge – teabag boxes

stagger like favelas on the shelf.
Boredom creeps its novelty into limbs

and out, into the limbs of trees.
The trees translate it. The sky collects

dropped apples. I ask the sky
some questions – it flashes back:

get used to nothing. I flinch, make pie
pour ink, occupy the paper pastry day

but nothing's heavenly, it swarms me
to the world. The time is time to lose.

NIGHT

Cold if you haven't the hang of laying fires.
No wifi or TV – monastic?

Not even a picture up. Just the cosmos –
and orange satin-clad whore mama

putting on another show. Red mascara'd
lids lowered, she sweeps in fishnets

from her cabriolet, salmon organza sliding
off, pooling over transfixed fields

where grasses lean in for a glimpse.
She adjusts her lace fascinator with lavender

kid gloves, is folded into the night's cold chest
cobalt intensifies to star-flecked black.

Disturbing Mother

If you're a dolt and sing insipid
songs to Nature, She'll eat you.

Like Ivan, you must demand
a hot bath, a hot dinner

then She'll wink, and you'll
get along just fine. She is an old

old hag, dripping with green
jewels, and She doesn't care

about you. She doesn't care
about Her gleaming yellow

toadstools, Her adorable fawns,
or Her resilient clumps of insect eggs.

She doesn't give a fig about this poem
I'm writing. She is writing the actual

poem. Full of scorn, wonder, acres
of scratch-black sky and trees.

Her scroll of references goes back
a hundred thousand years –

Her poem is breathing us alive.
Breathing us our sheepish

hesitations, our tender little egos,
our axe-wielding certainties.

But never thank Her.
She despises manners.

Who has time for those, when locked
in a permanent half-nelson by God?

Ghosts in the clearing

twist birch tambourine
ribbons, murmur backstage

choreograph grass
to ruffle in close-up

usher us in to observe
fact as the only awe.

Like our skins:
father-bark, girl-petal,

granny toadstool
in matt facepowder.

Tree-hosts bracket us
generations crane in.

Leaves halt and stiffen.
You leap in blue taffeta

camp as Hollywood
mime tea pouring

in a heaven of rustle.
The wind amplifies

our minds' applause.
But though everything

in the unforgettable world
creaks and bows –

you don't come back out.
We snail back through

crushed bracken, asking
if it's love or the theatre of it

that stabs and dazzles us
against our interminable dark.

Back to Earth

I load the dented greenie
with head-size bumping apples –
swerve them through Golders,
braking only for professors.

Gary, our teenager with ASD,
bounces out in khaki gaberdine,
bangs the gate, grabs
my flimsy green valise.

Our fence induces gasps:
newly painted tea-dance green.
Gary cranks open the boot,
gross metallic motor gesture –

out clunks the battering of apples.
A grasshopper, escaped here
from her rustic garrison, springs off
a meek fruit. *Greetings, greenie!*

I tip the hair-legged pet from my
cupped hands to Garizona.
Goggle of grasshopper eyes.
Tickle of grasshopper legs. Green

smell of gloss paint. Car-toxed apples.
Gary grins – briefly we're in league.
It's Friday, we're free, we're greenies!
Our shouts graffitti the street.

Canopy Lofty thoughts, highs and soaring visions. A sense of the divine, nests of red kites, crows, the place where the light hits, constant photosynthesis. Leaving all below sheltered? Making sure the others stay in the dark? How to rise above petty concerns, take the onslaught of rain, weather, war, judgement of the gods.

I've been spending a lot of time amongst trees — meditating alone and connecting with individual tree spirits.
The other day I spent so long on this I was surprised on looking down that I didn't have roots! That I could walk!
Georgiana, Norway —

I go birding with the man who re introduced the red kite into these woods. Once we we called to rescue a kite chick that had fallen out of its nest
My colleague had to climb up this huge oak returning the chick in a pop up garden bin!
Katie, Corby

Carmen,
ISLIP

When I first came to England I was
looking after 3 small boys – we were walking
along and saw this huge very old tree – the
boys RAN up to it and flung their arms
around its trunk! I caught them up and
they were whispering to the tree. I asked them
'What are you doing?' They said:"This is OUR SECRET
TREE, we tell it all our secrets and it never
tells them to anyone!"

Lola — Corby
at midnight on the summer solstice a few of us, old friends, go and celebrate with the trees
"Let our spirits soar!"

It's not that uncommon -
for kingfishers to land on
the rod - if you're sitting
in a reedbed, in a recess
they'll flit along, sometimes
land ~
Graham
Corby

We had a cousin the same age
as my brother who used to come
and stay — they didnt really get on although
my mum would always try and make
them play together

one time my
brother was sat at the table reading
his comic & mum looked a bit alarmed
"Where's Martin?"
"Oh — I took him to the woods and
we played cowboys and indians — I tied
him to a tree — I'll go and get him
later."

Suzy, Brigstock

I bought a field in a wood where I live – I was lucky and was offered six alpacas on the cheap. I love the quirkiness of these creatures! **They really make us laugh.** I've learnt to make felt from their wool – since David and I decided to take them on together, for my wedding dress. I've used Truffle's fleece to create the dreamy material – ROS, Fermyn Woods

I like climbing trees,
I think my
favourite food
at a picnic
would be cake.
If a deer came
and asked me
for some, I'd
give him a
crumb.

Jonty
BRIGSTOCK

We are lucky - we have the
woods right in our back garden -
we can hear the owls in the trees
as we go to sleep at night...
Nicola
Paddy
William
Bill
Weldon

clearing

Stumbling on peace,
a chance to rest,
allow something to
be revealed, replenish
the soul.
This is a gap, how
then to use it?
Can you bear to have
the sun stream down
on you?

Time to loosen the
nutty case you walk
around in, a grassy
place, sit down
and eat, reflect
and unmuddy the
thinking currents.

LOG JAM
I was in the woods one night with my trumpet just sitting on a log and this fox came up and said: "Hey! I've come here to sing! Mind if I bring my friends?" "Fine!" I said. They were hedgehogs who played drum on the logs.
William Weldon

How do you manage a woodland?
You manage the light! (Oh - same as how you manage a Painting or a Poem!)
I use the trees I manage in my woods for building. The old local houses are 12' deep - because that's the size of oak beam you can lift out of the forest.
ROB. Gretton

I like angels, and I like WOLVES!
I have seen a wolf before, but not in
these woods. What I like
about wolves is their colour, their
fur, and that they're a bit fierce —
what I like about angels is their wings.
I like the trees too.
HOLLIE, Wellingborough

I love the clearings - I like to just stand in them, stand still, listen and stare!

I've heard the first cuckoo of spring every year in Fernyhwoods - seen the first swallows to arrive - been transfixed by the buzzards swirling and whirling above - I'd love to come back as a buzzard!

Barbara Rounds

With kids on a council estate in Leicestershire we built a totem pole out of an oak. The young people have all the ideas on the projects I work on - that way they own it, they look after it, it all works! Once I'd taken all the scaffolding down I realised I'd left my cup of tea at the top!
Liam, Leicester

I found just the right art **workshop**
for all ages when I was doing the art att**ack**
thing at school— you dip a fir **cone** in glitter
and put a cardboard mount for a pot under it—
I went very purposefully to the woods to find
my pine cones— I walked for three hours,
getting lost (and scared, on my own) but I
ONLY FOUND FIVE PINE CONES!
when I came back I realised that I'd
actually LOVED my big scary walk in
the woods on my own!

MAIR, Brigstock

every animal is really my favourite — the deer, the butterflies, the squirrels, the red kites...
We've lived here in the woods about a year. I dont really like the bird shooters. I'm not keen on them. Its a shame we really have them in these woods.
JAy
Fermynwoods

I used to take my books and go and study up in Grafton underwood - there was nobody - it was completely quiet - total absence of noise: I'd sit in the fallen down WW2 bunkers - one day I looked up and there were two deer right in front of me.

We have a group of 60 volunteers
who, September to March come in
and help with coppicing - we have
a shop on site and we sell the wood
a lot for wood burning stoves
Lloyd. East Carlton

We were walking through the woods and we heard hammering — there was a group of guys who'd decided to build themselves a shed in the woods to live in! They had the frame up and everything!
Gary Corby

I love my job - the peace and quiet -
Yes, I've got one here - don't look! You
won't like it.
I shoot deer every day - they all go
off to the game dealer. It's part of my
work for the Forestry Commission, keeping
the numbers down.
SAM.
FERMYN WOODS

I get a lot of happiness from the woods, being in the woods with the trees. It wasn't always the case - but I'm learning - that I'm allowed to have an emotional reaction...
Keith,
Canning Town

You won't believe me, but I was out walking my dog — and I heard organ music! At 11.30 in the morning in the woods! I followed the sound... I came across a piano! It seemed to be playing this mysterious tune... I looked up and there were speakers in the trees. Well I went back several times — it was amazing!
Rachel, Lowick

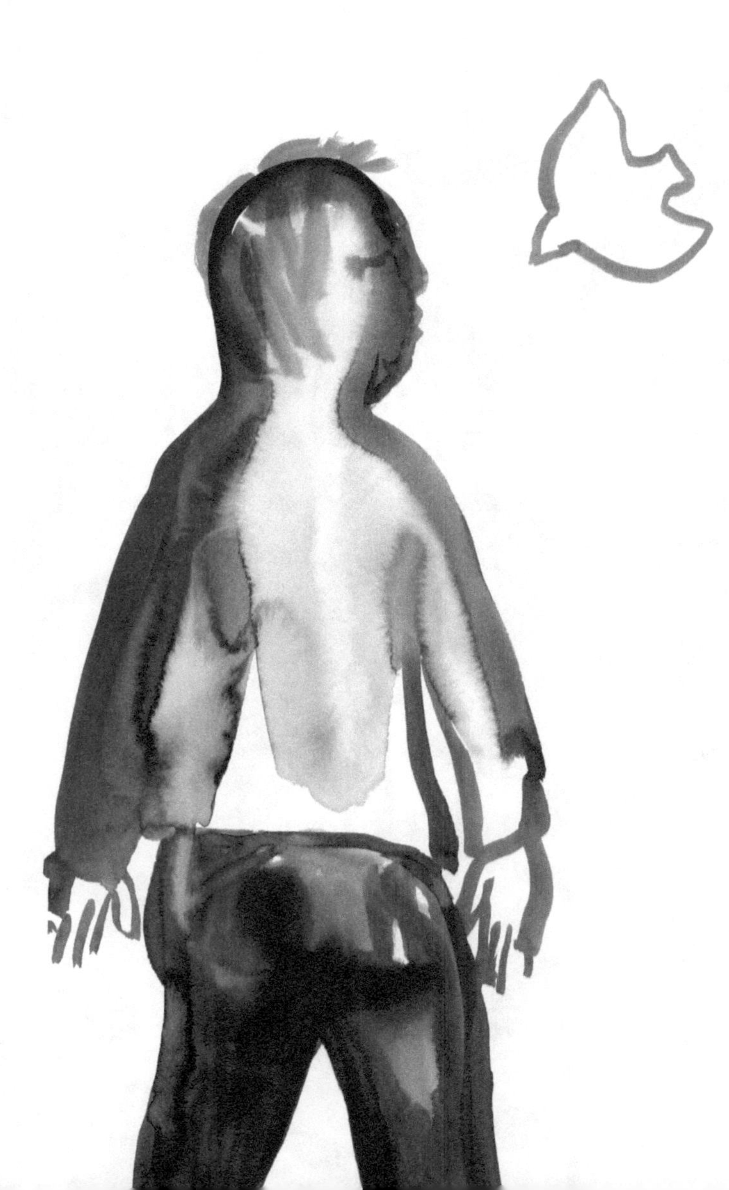

floor

Maggots make neat white stitches from earth to fallen crab apple. Decay ties us all together with everything else in this world. How to straddle the gulleys of mud, choose a ridge that will take the burden of human weight. Leaves, twigs, bluebells... after rain: populous fungi. Always texture: a crawling of the lower life forms, busy holding the world down flat so we can get across it. Eventually, lie in it.

The woods aren't so quiet — but
the rustling and the noises are good
for meditating — I like taking
photographs too — the contrast of
a dead tree in the middle of the alive
ones — providing all that support for
life, the fungi, the insects, the animals
that feed on the insects. Michael,
Corby

#

Mel
&
Jude
we work in logistics
like so many light deprived
mushrooms and toadstools
growing in a dark cupboard
There are about forty of us but
we are the beautiful truffles —
most of the others are poisonous!
Mel & Jude, Corby

We were out in the woods
with artist Martin Prothero, and
he was showing us animal tracks,
one he called 'the superhighway' - a
path made by deer and then used by
all the little animals.

He was talking about plants and
how things that work well together often
grow together "I've been drinking a lot
of Dandelion and Burdock" said Nat -
"there's the dandelion... where's the burdock?"
"It's behind you!" said Martin!

Gareth ~
CORBY
I've been away for seven years — running bars in Gran Canaria for five years, then in Norway for two — now I'm back in Corby trying to spend time away from my laptop — clearing away beercans instead of serving them up!

I really like looking under rocks - sometimes you see all the ants wriggling about - all sorts of creepy crawlies!
I like doing this by myself. nice & peaceful!
Oscar, BRIGSTOCK

yes, they're everywhere —
you don't even need rain —
just a little mizzle.

John, Corby

www.ingramcontent.com/pod-product-compliance
Lightning Source LLC
Chambersburg PA
CBHW050759080726
47590CB00021B/3135